Longman Structural Readers: Background
Stage 1

London

Leslie Dunkling

Pearson Education Limited
Edinburgh Gate, Harlow,
Essex CM20 2JE, England
and Associated Companies throughout the world.

© Longman Group Limited 1984

First published 1984
Eighteenth impression Penguin Books 1999

ISBN 0-582-74905-0

Acknowledgements
We should like to thank the following for their permission
to use copyright photographs:
Daily Telegraph Colour Library (Audrey Stirling) for title
page; Elizabeth Photo Library for pages 4 (left), 5 (above
right), 12 (above), 20 (above), 23 (below left), 28 (below)
and 30 (right); Patrick Thurston for pages 4 (above right),
21 (below), 22 (above left), 29 (above left) and 31 (below
left); Darryl Williams for pages 4 (below right, 10, 11, 19
(below) and 31 (above); Robert Estall for pages 5 (left), 14
(below left), 20 (below), 25 (left), 26 and 28 (above); Brian
Shuel for pages 5 (below right), 15 (below) and 18 (above);
British Tourist Authority for pages 8, 9, 12 (below), 14
(above), 16, 18 (below), 19 (above), 21 (above), 22 (above
right and below), 23 (above and below right), 24, 27, 29
(right), 30 (above left) and 31 (below right); Aerofilms for
page 13; Controller of Her Britannic Majesty's Stationery
Office for page 15 (above) British Crown copyright; Burke
Fotografic for page 17; Robert Harding Picture Library for
page 25 (right) and Madame Tussaud's for page 29 (below
left).

Printed in China
GCC/18

Contents

Welcome to London!

In this book we welcome you to London. London is a big city, and big cities are not always different. Modern buildings, modern shops and stores, hotels and cinemas are not different in today's cities. But some things are different in every city. This book asks: "What is different in London? What things can you see only in London?"

In London – the different city – you find Beefeaters and Pearly Kings and Queens. You find Covent Garden and Madame Tussaud's. You find the Houses of Parliament, with Big Ben beside them. You see London's occasions and ceremonies.

What are Beefeaters, and who are the Pearly Kings and Queens? What can you see in Madame Tussaud's? The answers to those questions are in this book. Here is London. Welcome!

REGENT'S PARK

Madame
Tussaud's

Post Office Tower

British Museum

Marble Arch

OXFORD ST

REGENT ST

SOHO

Covent Garden

National
Gallery

PICCADILLY
CIRCUS

TRAFALGAR SQUARE

HYDE
PARK

PARK LANE

PICCADILLY

GREEN PARK

THE MALL

ST JAMES'S PARK

Westminster Abbey

Westmins

Houses of
Parliament

Buckingham Palace

Lambeth Br

WESTMINSTER

N
W E
S

St Paul's Cathedral

Bank of England

CITY

The Monument

Tower of London

FLEET ST

St Mary-le-Bow

BANK

Blackfriars Br

RIVER THAMES

Southwark Br

Mansion House

London Br

National Theatre

Tower Br

A map of central London

0   ½   I KILOMETRE

Royal London

London is a royal city. The British king or queen has a palace there – Buckingham Palace. Queen Elizabeth lives there now. Important visitors often go to the palace. They meet Queen Elizabeth and the royal family inside the palace.

Tourists go to Buckingham Palace too, but they don't go inside, and they don't meet the queen. They stand outside and see the *Changing of the Guard*. There are always guardsmen outside the palace. Every day a new guard of thirty guardsmen marches to the palace and takes the place of the "old guard". That is the "changing of the guard".

▲ A guardsman and the new guard   *One guardsman is near us in this photograph. The new guard is here now. You can see the new guard – a line of guardsmen in their red coats. The tourists are outside.*

The changing of the guard is not a big ceremony. London has important royal ceremonies too. The State Opening of Parliament and the Trooping of the Colour are two of these.

The *State Opening of Parliament* (below) is the queen's visit to the Houses of Parliament. She goes there in one of the royal coaches. Hundreds of people watch the procession.

The queen does not go in a coach to the *Trooping of the Colour* (below). She rides there, and she watches the ceremony from her horse. The "colour" is a flag. The guards "troop" (march with) the colour for the queen.

The Trooping of the Colour
One regiment of foot guards and one regiment of horse guards march past the queen. The "colour" is the flag of the regiment of foot guards. ▼

◀
One of the royal coaches at the State Opening of Parliament.

Royal occasions

The British people like the queen and the royal family. They like important occasions too.

A royal wedding is always a big occasion. The royal family go to the wedding in a procession, and people love processions. The people watch the procession, and they see the royal family in their coaches. Horse guards ride with the coaches, and the procession goes between lines of foot guards along the road.

▲ A royal wedding *Lady Diana Spencer comes in a coach to St Paul's Cathedral. She comes with her father. Prince Charles is waiting inside St Paul's. Hundreds of important people are inside the cathedral. Thousands of people are outside. They are going to wait and see the prince and the princess after the wedding.*

The prince and princess leave St Paul's Cathedral after their wedding. ▶

Street parties give children a day to remember.

The Jubilee (25 years) of Queen Elizabeth II – queen of the United Kingdom from 1952 to 1977. The Jubilee is a big ceremony. Important people come to London from every part of the world.

But our pictures are not of important people. This is a street party. The people of this London street are having a party. The party is on the day of the Jubilee, and it's a Jubilee party. But it isn't for important people. It's for the people of the street. The children of this street are going to remember the Jubilee.

11

Westminster

Tourists in London always want to visit Westminster and see "Big Ben". They want to see the clock in its tower, and they want to hear the bells.

"Big Ben" is really a bell. You hear it at every hour. It is the big bell (13,720 kilograms) with a deep voice, and it counts the hours. You hear its deep voice on the radio: "This is the BBC. The time is six o'clock." And you hear the deep BOOM of Big Ben six times.

Big Ben.

The famous clock tower stands beside the Houses of Parliament. The country's leaders speak in the Houses of Parliament. The men and women there are the voice of the British people. The people choose 650 men and women for the House of Commons. The second "House" is the House of Lords. The men and women in it are the dukes, earls, and lords of the great families, heads of the Church of England, head judges, and some modern "Life Peers" and "Life Peeresses". These two "Houses" are the Parliament.

The Houses of Parliament.

The Thames from the air *This is a good photograph of Westminster from a helicopter. Look at the map on pages 6 and 7. What places can you name?* ▼

Westminster Bridge is one bridge across the River Thames in London. Look at the map on pages 6 and 7, and find the bridges.

Big Ben and the Houses of Parliament stand beside the River Thames. You can go on a boat from Westminster and see London from the river.

The Tower of London

Tower Bridge is one of the famous bridges across the Thames. It is near the Tower of London. You can see the buildings of the Tower from the river.

The Tower is old, and it has a long and cruel history. It is not only one building. The tall building in the picture is the White Tower.

The Bloody Tower is near the river. You do not see blood there today, but the Bloody Tower has a history of blood – the blood of men, women and children.

Are there ghosts in the Tower? People say, "The ghosts of famous men and women walk in the Tower of London. You often see the ghosts of Anne Boleyn and Lady Jane Grey in the night."

The Tower of London is not a place of blood now. It *is* an interesting place, with its Beefeaters and the Crown Jewels.

Tower Bridge (*above*) *It opens, and then ships can go up or down the river.*

◄ *The Tower of London.*

The Imperial State Crown is one of the Crown Jewels in the Jewel House in the Tower of London. It has 3,000 stones in it: diamonds, red rubies, blue sapphires, and beautiful pearls. The queen wears it on state occasions. Then it goes back to the Tower.

The Imperial State Crown. ▲

The "Beefeaters" are soldiers. Their real name is Yeoman Warders of the Tower. Their clothes are the clothes of royal guards of the year 1500. The Beefeaters guard the Tower and the Crown Jewels, and they help visitors. Guardsmen of today, from a regiment of foot guards, are always there too.

◄

Yeoman Warders of the Tower.

London's ceremonies

London has important ceremonies. Some are every day and some are every year. At the Tower of London is the *Ceremony of the Keys*. The keys in this ceremony lock the gates of the Tower. In the photograph, the Chief Warder of the Tower is carrying the keys. With four modern guardsmen, he marches to the gates and locks them. Then he takes the keys to the Governor of the Tower. This ceremony is at ten o'clock every night. It is a very old ceremony – 700 years old.

The Ceremony of the Keys. ▲

The *Lord Mayor's Show* is an old ceremony, too. The people of the City of London choose a Lord Mayor every year. And every year they see him in the Lord Mayor's Show. The Lord Mayor's coach takes him to the Mansion House in a long procession (below). The procession is the show – the Lord Mayor's Show.

The new Lord Mayor in his coach. ▶

London's churches

You can see a number of London's famous churches from the river. St Paul's Cathedral is not very near the river, but it stands at the top of Ludgate Hill. You can see it from the river in the photograph on page 5. You can go up to the top of the cathedral. You go up 627 steps from the floor of the cathedral to the top.

Westminster Abbey is near the Houses of Parliament. It is near the Thames, too, and you can see its two towers from the river. It is old (1042–1065) and very big (158 metres long).

Westminster Abbey. ▶

◀ *The "new" St Paul's Cathedral dates from 1675. (See* London's history *on page 32.)*

Cockneys

A large number of the London churches have bells. The small church of St Mary-le-Bow is between St Paul's Cathedral and the Bank of England. It is the Cockney church. A "Cockney" is a Londoner, but not every Londoner is a real Cockney. The real Cockneys can hear Bow bells – the bells of St Mary-le-Bow – from their houses.

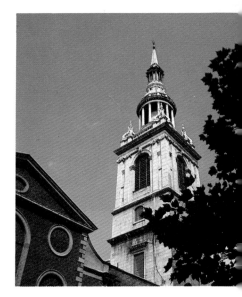

St Mary-le Bow – the Cockney church. ▶

Pearlies – the Cockney royal family.

The United Kingdom has only one Royal Family, but the Cockneys have their pearly "kings and queens". The pearly kings and queens take their name from the pearly buttons on their clothes. They work in London's street markets, and they are the "kings" and "queens" of the market people. But they do not dress in their pearly clothes every day.

19

Petticoat Lane – the Cockney market.

Markets

London has its famous shops and big stores. But its street markets are the really interesting places.

In Portobello Road they sell old things – old, but interesting. It is a collectors' market. Look at the people. Is that old man a collector? Yes. He has a collection of old matchboxes. This is the market for him: there are old matchboxes in two or three of the shops. Is this young woman a collector? No, but her mother has a collection of old pictures from China. Portobello Road is the place for them.

Petticoat Lane, in the City, is the Cockney market.

Portobello Road – the collectors' market.

Go there on a Sunday morning, and perhaps you can see a Pearly King and a Pearly Queen. The Cockneys of Petticoat Lane sell new things. Perhaps you don't really want those things, but the Cockneys in Petticoat Lane can sell them to you!

20

Covent Garden today.

Covent Garden is famous. But the very old fruit and vegetable market is not there now. The big trucks take the fruit and the vegetables to a new market near the Thames. Without the trucks and the market, Covent Garden is a different place. But it is a busy place. It has new shops and cafés. You can sit at a café table and listen to music. You can meet friends and sit in the sun – or sit out of the rain in the old market buildings.

The old Covent Garden market.

Meet some Londoners

▲ *A London policeman* with a young visitor.

▲ *A Chelsea pensioner* The 360 Chelsea pensioners are old soldiers. They live in the Royal Hospital near the Thames at Chelsea. In the months of June, July and August the pensioners wear long red coats. In the cold months they wear thick blue coats.

▲ *The buskers* These two girls are buskers. They play music in the street and people give money to them.

◀ *The speaker* There are speakers every Sunday in Hyde Park, and every day near the Tower of London.

▲ *The commissionaire* He is an old soldier. He works at the door of the *Dorchester* hotel.

▲ *"Fares, please"* The conductress on the big red London bus helps you, and takes your fare.

▲ *The taxi driver* Say the name of a street in London. He knows it, and he can take you there. (There are 20,000 streets in London.)

◄ *The street performer* It's nice to stop in the street and watch a street performer.

23

The City

London is a city, but to Londoners "the City" is a place *in*
London. St Paul's Cathedral is in the City, and the banks
and big companies have their head offices there. City offices
are in tall modern buildings, or in old buildings on narrow
streets. The office people do not live in the City; they come
to the City every day, from Monday to Friday. Only 5,890
people *live* in the City; 340,000 people *work* there. They
come in trains, on buses, on the Underground, on bicycles,
and in cars and taxis. They come in one hour – "rush hour".
Rush hour is from 8.30 to 9.30 in the morning, and the
evening rush hour is from 5.00 to 6.00.

A City worker   *This man works
in a bank in the City. His dark
suit, bowler hat and black
umbrella are not a uniform, but
you can see a large number of men
in the City with suits, bowler hats
and umbrellas.*

St Paul's Cathedral is near the middle of the City. Perhaps
the real middle is "the Bank". Seven streets meet at the
Bank. The Bank of England is there – with the British
Government's money in it. The Royal Exchange is there; it
is not now the British money market, but it is a beautiful
building. The Mansion House is there too. The Mansion
House is the office and house of the Lord Mayor of London.

The Monument *is near the Bank. It is at the place of the first fire in the Great Fire of London. (See the year 1666 in* London's history *on page 32.)* ▶

The Royal Exchange *The building behind it is the head office of a bank.* ▼

UNDERGROUND
BANK STATION

A "night out" in the West End

Five important streets meet at Piccadilly Circus in London's "West End". The cars, the tourist coaches, the red London buses, and the taxis go round a statue there.

It is not the statue of a famous man or woman. People don't remember the statue's real name. They say: "It's Eros, the Greek god of love."

Under the road, two Underground lines meet. Piccadilly Circus is a very busy place. It is busy day and night. People come here to the shops in the day time, and at night they come for a night out.

Piccadilly Circus at night *You can't see the hundreds of people. They are there, but they are moving. You see the lights of cars and buses, but you don't see the cars and buses. They are moving too. The statue of Eros is on the right.*

A London pub It is a place for good beer (or a "soft drink" – coca-cola etc.) and good conversation.

Londoners like a night out in the West End. They take the Underground to Piccadilly Circus, and there they are in the middle of the West End.

They can eat in one of the restaurants in the West End near Piccadilly Circus. They can get food from twenty different countries in West End restaurants.

Londoners, and visitors, can go to a theatre in the West End, or to a concert, to an opera or a ballet. And there are fifty cinemas near Piccadilly Circus.

Or they can have a good "night out" in a pub – conversation and a drink or two.

A London theatre in the West End.

Libraries, museums and art galleries

The British Library has 10,000,000 books in London. The Reading Room of the library is famous. That's only one library. London has hundreds of small libraries.

▲ *The British Museum*

The British Museum is famous, but young people often go to the museums in Kensington. In the British Museum, you look at things, but in the Kensington museums you can *do* things.

The National Gallery and the Tate Gallery are the two big London art galleries. They have some very famous pictures in them. You can see the history of British art in the Tate Gallery beside the Thames. London has small galleries too. They often have exhibitions of famous pictures from galleries in Europe and America.

The National Gallery   *In this picture you are seeing it from Trafalgar Square. Nelson's Column (55 metres high) is in Trafalgar Square – and hundreds of very fat pigeons. The pigeons get food from the tourists, but the National Gallery does not like pigeons on its roof or outside its windows.* ▼

Exhibitions and shows

You can see a new exhibition or a show every week in London. Some of the London shows are famous. People come to them from many countries.

People like different things, and London has exhibitions of cars, boats, books, pictures, food, clothes, bicycles . . .

There is a famous dog show in London every year. It is Crufts Dog Show. People watch it on television. They see many dogs – and their owners.

Madame Tussaud's is famous too – for waxworks. There are waxworks of famous people (good and bad) in Madame Tussaud's waxworks show. You see not only people of the past but famous people of today there: kings, queens, princes and princesses, sportsmen and sportswomen, cinema stars and pop stars.

▲ *The Chelsea Flower Show takes place every May.*

Crufts Dog Show. ▲

◄ *Elvis Presley at Madame Tussaud's.*

29

You can sit by the lake in St ▲
James's Park – on a good day.

◄ A bandstand in a London
park   *In the summer, a band
plays here every afternoon. It is
often the band of a famous
regiment.*

London's parks and gardens

Londoners like the parks. Office workers often sit in them
and eat their lunch. Bands play at lunchtime and in the
afternoon.

Hyde Park is famous, but it is only one of London's big
parks. You can see the big parks on the map of London
(pages 6–7). Come to London one day and walk in them.
The parks are open to the people, but the big parks are really
royal parks.

Regent's Park has the London zoo, with the animals of the
world. And in the summer it has an open-air theatre. You
can sit in a chair or on the grass, and you see a play between
the trees. The play is always by Shakespeare.

London has small parks and gardens too. You can walk in
them, sit in them, play in them, take boats on the water in
them – on good days in summer.

A "sea" of flowers in Kensington Gardens – opposite the Albert Hall.

Shakespeare in the open air. ▲
People enjoy Much Ado About
Nothing *in Regent's Park's
theatre.*

◀ *A winter's afternoon in Hyde
Park, London.*

London's history

Year

AD	43	The Romans come to London. They build a bridge across the Thames.
	410	The Romans leave London.
	604	London workmen build the first St Paul's Cathedral.
	1066	William the Conqueror comes to England from Normandy in France. In Westminster Abbey he takes the English crown.
	1081–1097	Workmen build the White Tower at the Tower of London.
	1348–1349	10,000 Londoners die in a plague – the "Black Death".
	1476	William Caxton prints his first book in London.
	1577	The first real theatre opens in London.
	1649	Execution of King Charles I in London.
	1660	The people want a king again. Charles II comes to London.
	1665	Death comes to London again. 100,000 Londoners die in the "Great Plague".
	1666	The Great Fire of London. London loses St Paul's Cathedral and 88 churches in a big fire.
	1675–1711	Workmen build a new St Paul's Cathedral.
	1694	The Bank of England opens in the City of London.
	1759	The British Museum opens in London.
	1801	The population of London is 864,000.
	1829	Sir Robert Peel puts the first policemen on London streets.
	1836	London's first railway station opens.
	1863	The first underground trains run in London.
	1881	The population of London is now 3,330,000.
	1952	Elizabeth II is the new queen.
	1961	The population of London is 8,000,000
	1983	The population of London is 6,700,000. People are moving out of central London.